The True Story of
Miracle Man

Lois Szymanski

Schiffer Publishing Ltd®

4880 Lower Valley Road • Atglen, PA 19310

Chapter One

The sun was round and full and hot. Wicked rays hammered the frail foal. He stretched his spindly front legs out under the leaves of a nearby myrtle bush, finding cool shade for his hooves and forelegs. The pain in his back leg throbbed, but the colt was tired and the only way to rest meant he had to tuck the sore leg under him...where the weight of his body only added to the pain.

A haze of black flies buzzed circles around him, landing again and again to take pricking painful bites. He shook his head in frustration, but the mane was too short and fuzzy to shoo insects away, so he closed his eyes and listened to the sounds of the marsh.

When it was quiet like this, with just the sound of water slapping and frogs peeping and the call of a gull in the distance, he could recall the warm breath of his mother. He could almost remember how her moist tongue felt on his neck and how she had whuffed warm sweet air onto his face. She was gone now, though. He'd left her body a day ago, stumbling along the path of hoofprints made by the herd that had left them far behind.

There had been warm milk just after his birth, rich liquid that spilled over his tongue, down his throat and into his tummy, making it feel round and full. Now there was none... and his empty stomach rumbled.

"Over there, Myrna! Isn't that a foal?"

His eyes flew open with the sound. He'd never heard voices like that and it frightened him. He blinked rapidly to calm the sore spot in his eye and looked across the ribbon of murky water where two humans stood on the roadway. The woman put binoculars to her face.

"Yes, I see him... a tiny brown and white pinto. Wait a minute... he's actually a tri-color. I see black in his mane." She panned the binoculars over the area and back again. "Oh Bob, he's all alone. There's not another pony in sight!" Her voice was full with tones the foal didn't recognize.

"We've got to let someone know."

Her voice sent waves of fear through the foal and he scrambled to his feet, bracing to hold himself erect. Across the water, the woman paced back and forth on the roadway.

"I wonder what happened to his mother?" The woman's voice sounded sad, but it also had an alarm inside it — a sound like the stallion used when he wanted to make the herd run — and that frightened the colt.

"Now, Myrna. Don't worry." The man patted her back gently. "We'll go on over to the Refuge Inn and let Arthur know. He'll know what to do."

"Yes, yes. That's a good idea." The woman spun and headed for the navy blue car parked on the side of the road. "Come on, Bob. No time to fool around."

The colt watched them get into the car and drive away. He'd heard and seen cars pass by throughout the day. Now he knew what was inside them and he wondered if humans were dangerous. His fuzzy ears perked up. He listened until the sound of their engine faded into nothing again.

A Canada goose honked across the way. The water exploded when the flock rose into the air, wings flapping. A tall heron with legs as thin as reeds raised his head from fishing in the water and watched the geese form a V overhead, flying toward the line of loblolly pines. The colt observed it all...and then he folded his legs and sank to the ground once more. When he closed his eyes, he could remember his momma.

A man hurried across the road from the old Suburban he had crookedly parked. He shaded his eyes against the ball of orange sun setting in the sky. His eyes settled on the foal whose body poked out from under the myrtle bush.

The foal watched the man warily. It hadn't been long since the other two humans left. They had only looked, but this one was coming his way.

The man slid down the bank and called out. "Hey little one, are you okay?"

The colt raised his head. His eyes rolled in fear and he snorted. The sound was low and grumbling.

The man pushed his way through tall cattails and waded right into the water, fully clothed. The water was deep, up to his knees, his waist, and then his chest. A moment later he was out of the water, covered in muck and mud, and heading right for the foal.

The colt raised himself, standing on shaky legs, and stared. Fear enveloped him. He felt he had to get away, but he was tired and weak. The image of the man blurred and spun before him.

The man moved closer, his hand outstretched. "Come on little boy. Where's your momma? Come to Arthur. We'll take care of you."

When Arthur finally reached him, a burst of life jolted through the colt and he bolted away...just out of the man's reach.

"Now, come on," Arthur said. "You'll never make it out here on your own. You need warm milk and food to survive. You need someone to protect you." His voice was gentle, sing-songy, and soft.

This time, Arthur's outstretched hand had almost touched the colt's muzzle before the brown and white body shot away again.

The colt's legs shook with exhaustion. He held his head up and watched the man. He snorted and shook his forelock. His mane bobbed and flecks of dried mud flew sideways from his body. The man laughed.

"Baby boy, you'll die out here alone," Arthur warned. The colt trotted off, another few feet away, around the myrtle bushes and golden brown reeds.

Again and again, Arthur tried to catch the foal, but each time the determined baby raced away, just out of reach.

The sun dropped lower in the sky. Darkness settled over Assateague Island.

Arthur sat back on his heels. His hand was still outstretched. He shook his head. Each time he'd drawn close, the colt had skittered away.

Finally, Arthur turned and waded back into the water and across the mucky marsh. "I'm not leaving you," he told the colt. "Not yet."

The colt watched as the man scrambled out of the water and up the bank on the other side.

Arthur reached into the cab of his truck and pulled out a telephone, held it to his ear, and spoke. In the still of evening, Arthur's voice carried across the water.

"We've got an orphan colt out here," he said. "Bring the fire truck and a small boat. I'm at Black Duck Marsh."

The foal watched. He raised his nose in the air and whinnied. The sound was long and lonesome and it carried across the marshes.

"He's calling for his momma," Arthur said, "but she's nowhere in sight." He paused. "When you get here, park the truck so the headlights shine across the water. We're going to have to bring him through it."

The colt watched the man put the silver thing into his pocket and lean against the bumper of the truck. Mosquitoes and horseflies buzzed around his fuzzy ears. By now, he was used to their humming. He barely felt the sting anymore. He'd been bitten so many times he'd given up trying to chase them away. He was so tired.

Soon, the colt's legs buckled and he lowered himself to the ground, resting his head on his forelegs, watching the man. Frogs chirped. A goose honked. A picture of his mother filled his head and he snorted, soft and low. All he could do was wait.

Courtesy of Brenda Boonie.

Chapter Two

It wasn't long until the colt heard a rumble like thunder. It grew louder as a large truck approached, spun gravel, and slid into a spot, parking behind the man's car on the side of the road. Three men tumbled from the bright red vehicle.

"Whatcha got there, Arthur?" one of them said, his voice booming across the expanse.

The sun had set. It was hard for the colt to see the shadowy figures on the bank, but he saw them pull a shiny vessel from the side of the truck.

One of the men slapped Arthur on the back. "It looks like you did fine without the boat," he said, laughing and pointing at Arthur's muddy legs and his sopping shoes.

"Yeah, yeah," Arthur retorted as he pushed the boat toward the bank. "I tried and I failed. You would have done the same thing."

The men looked across the water at the colt and silence fell. Arthur slid the boat into the water and another man climbed in with him.

The colt heard the slap, slap of a paddle in the water. He watched the silver-colored craft draw close and his heart thumped faster.

Arthur slid muddy legs into the water and pulled the boat ashore. Both men stepped out.

The foal was tired, but he scrambled to stand. This time it took him three tries to get up. When the two men reached him, the spotted foal drew strength from deep inside, finding the energy to dart away.

The men were silhouettes before the bright lights that shone across the water. Their shadowy shapes frightened the spotted colt. His blood raced faster than his legs could carry him. Arthur was almost upon him. Mud flew from tiny black hooves as the colt shot away.

"Ha ha ha!" Across the canal, the man sitting on the hood of the fire engine laughed out loud at Arthur and his friend.

The colt's fear doubled when he heard the voice echoing over the water. He leapt sideways. Hands reached out, grabbing from all sides. He shot behind a myrtle bush, and from there to a scrub pine and then to a thick line of tall pampas grass. The men were hot on his trail, one on the right and one on the left. They spread their arms wide and herded him toward the line of reeds and cattails, cornering him.

The colt threw his head into the air and whinnied, a pitiful squeal that echoed in the misty night air. Muscular arms came around his furry neck and he gave in to the fear, collapsing on the ground in a bundle of mud and legs.

"Poor little guy," Arthur said. He huffed and puffed with exhaustion. His thick arms slipped around the colt's midsection and he hauled the baby to his feet.

The other man still had his arms around the colt's neck. "He's a bag of bones," he said, his voice full of wonder. "How'd he find the energy to move like that?"

Arthur shook his head. "He sure gave us a run for the money," he agreed. "Let's get him in the boat. We need to call Doc Cameron."

"In the boat? Are you sure? He'll tip us over if he goes nuts. Maybe we should walk him through the water."

Arthur ran rough fingers through the fuzzy black and white mane, tenderly working globs of mud from fine hair. "He's about done in," he said. "I think he'll be fine."

They walked to the boat, one on either side of the colt. Arthur lifted him inside. Tiny hooves clanked against the metal boat's bottom. The colt crumbled and tucked his legs under himself. He struggled when Arthur held him tight, but the man was strong. He closed his eyes and gave in to the fear, still but alert. He could feel the boat gliding across the canal. It was an odd sensation, but he was too tired to fight anymore.

In his mind, he saw the warm brown and white form of his mother. He remembered the feel of milk rushing over his tongue and down his throat. He felt her swishing tail sweep flies from his face...and then he remembered two days of stinging insects and horrifying night sounds. Maybe leaving the marsh behind was a good thing.

"We can take him in my truck." The voice jarred the colt. A man with shaggy grey hair was talking. "Over to your dad's place?" he asked.

Arthur nodded. He scooped the colt up in his arms, stepped up the bank, and hoisted him into the back of the pickup truck, climbing in beside him.

The man with gray hair shut the tailgate.

"Drive slow," Arthur said. "He may look plumb tuckered out, but I've seen this colt explode out of a near dead body. There's no telling when it could happen again."

"I've never lost a patient," the man joked, his back to them when he hopped in the cab of his truck and slammed the door.

The colt cringed at every odd sound, but Arthur's arms were as dense as tree trunks and they were wrapped firmly around his neck and midsection.

"You're gonna be fine," the man said. He leaned closer. Stubble from his red beard brushed the colt's ears. Arthur's voice was deep and raspy, but he spoke slowly and his warm tone calmed and soothed the colt. "We're going get you all better, boy."

The colt laid his head in Arthur's huge palm and closed his eyes. He was done with fighting. His leg throbbed. His eye felt like it had a lump of briars in it, jabbing away at the eyelid. His stomach grumbled with angry hunger pains. How could it get worse?

The truck moved slowly down the beach road, following the fire engine. A strong breeze whipped over the bed of the truck. The colt smelled rain in the air. It had rained the night he was born. His mother had sheltered him from fat crystal droplets, hanging her shaggy head over his body, licking water from the white blaze that ran down his face. Tall pine trees swayed and bent with each gust of wind and their shadows danced like monsters on the roadway.

Arthur stroked the colt's white shoulders. He scratched the black forelock that stood up like a Mohawk and worked his way down the line of fuzzy mane to where it turned white. He gently stroked brown patches crisscrossing the foal's body and circled with a finger the freckles that spattered the white parts of his coat. "You sure are marked pretty," Arthur said. His voice was like velvet.

The colt liked the sing-songy sound of the voice. He liked the feel of strong hands rubbing his body. It made him feel safe.

Thunder rumbled behind them, somewhere out on the ocean. The colt trembled, but Arthur did not waver beside him.

The truck crossed the causeway from Assateague Island onto Chincoteague. The driver wound down his window. "You okay back there," he yelled.

"Yeah," Arthur said. "After we get this colt settled in a stall, will you take me back over to get my truck?"

The gray haired man laughed. "Yeah, but it'll cost you."

"I'll get the morning coffee," Arthur countered.

They reached a stop sign at Main Street. The truck turned right. The colt opened his eyes and then closed them. Opened them and then closed them again. He wanted to see where they were going, but he was so tired. He wanted to sleep, but his eye hurt too much to stay closed. He felt mixed up.

Chincoteague Bay stretched out to the left of them. They motored down Main Street, past the high school on the right, and past a decoy shop on the left. They stopped to wait for a mother duck and her line of ducklings to cross the road in front of the truck.

Where am I going? the colt wondered. What will happen to me? His stomach rumbled and he wondered one more thing. Will I ever taste warm milk again?

The truck slowed and the road turned to gravel. They entered the lane to Arthur's family farm. Chincoteague Pony Farm had been in the family for generations. It encompassed the entire northern tip of Chincoteague Island. Ponies grazing on marsh grasses all the way out to where the land met the water raised their heads and watched. One of them whinnied and trotted along the fence.

Several older barns and outbuildings sat crookedly on the left side of the road across from a large white clapboard house on the right. The pickup truck eased into a parking area next to one of the barns and stopped. The gray-haired man hopped out and opened the tailgate.

Arthur scooted forward out of the bed and onto the truck's tailgate. He wrapped those long, warm arms around the colt and scooped him up again.

The colt let his body hang limp, riding all the way into the barn where Arthur deposited him into a bed of thick straw. He watched Arthur stretch. He didn't want the man to leave him and he struggled to stand in the knee-deep, golden grass. The ground had never felt so soft. He did not know where he was and he did not know what would become of him. All he knew was that he was no longer on Assateague Island. He was far from the rest of the herd and his mother, and he was alone.

Courtesy of Carol Gazunis.

Chapter Three

"You wait here," Arthur told the colt. "Hang on 'til I get back." He opened the stall door and slipped out.

The colt struggled to stand, but this time his legs would not cooperate. He thrashed in the straw, weak and exhausted. His little hooves scrambled, sliding in the sawdust beneath the straw. He rolled his eyes, begging, *Don't leave me. I don't want to be alone again.*

As if reading the colt's mind, Arthur spoke. "You are warm and safe here," he said, "and I won't be long."

The barn door closed with a whoosh. Darkness settled over the colt. His heart fluttered furiously. Here, no marsh sounds comforted him. He listened for the call of a loon or the cackle of a gull, but there was none. He strained his fuzzy ears to hear tree frogs chirping or the sound of a fish slapping the water, but all he heard was the scratch, scratch, scratch of a mouse making a bed in the corner of the stall.

Light sifted through a window pane high in the corner of the barn. It cast a swath of golden light across the straw, touching the colt's forelegs. He dipped his head to stare at the light reflecting from his tiny hooves. The storm had rumbled out to sea and the moon was high in the night sky. Something magical was happening. He could feel it in his bones. Arthur had brought some sort of magic to him.

The colt settled deep in the straw. He rolled on his side, stretched out his legs and rested his head in golden-lit straw. He closed his eyes and finally, the colt slept.

Click! The colt's head shot up. The barn door opened. His bunched nerves settled. The cobwebs of sleep were swept from his brain when he realized Arthur was back.

"Okay, little guy," Arthur said. He whooshed into the stall, plunking a bag and a sloshing bucket of water down beside the colt. "Let's see about your wounds, and then we've got to get some milk into you."

The colt thrashed again, trying to stand. It was no use.

Arthur's hand came down, soft on the foal's neck. He felt a warm, wet tongue stroke him, kind and comforting...then he realized it wasn't a tongue.

"There, there, little one," Arthur's voice pacified the foal as he stroked the colt's face lightly with a rag dipped in warm water. He scrubbed mud from the little one's neck, moving down to the shoulder and chest. Carefully, he wiped away traces of Assateague, replacing the colt's memories of forlorn nights without his momma with a realization that he was no longer alone.

Arthur dipped the rag back into the bucket, wringing it out before tackling muddy forelegs. He moved onto the rear legs and then stopped to stare at a gaping abscess in the rear right leg. It was red and inflamed and oozed yellow pus. "Oh, boy," Arthur muttered. "That can't be good."

Carefully, he cleaned the wound, dipping the rag into the bucket again and again, scraping away mud and dried blood.

The colt winced with pain, but didn't fight the man. He knew now that Arthur was taking care of him. Contact sent shock waves up his leg, but at the same time the rag was warm and soothing... It reminded him of his mother's soft tongue.

Arthur finished cleaning the bad leg and moved to the last. The water in the bucket was no longer clean. It was murky and brown like marsh waters after the tide had gone out. Arthur looked in each ear, smiled, and then took the colt's head in his hands, tilting it upward so he could look into his eyes.

The colt tried to hold the man's gaze, but his sore eye blinked and burned.

Arthur's smile disappeared. "Dang it, boy. You've got an abscess in your eye, too. The insects must have had a field day while you lay out there all alone." He stroked the colt's neck and ran a finger down his nose, tracing the white blaze. "Don't worry," he said. "Tomorrow, we'll get you fixed up."

The colt stared at the man with his good eye. Arthur's face was round and ruddy with a full red beard. His blue eyes were soft and kind. Something about the big man was reassuring and the colt felt safe for the first time in a long time.

Arthur reached into the bag next to the water bucket and pulled out a bottle with a soft nipple on the end. "This is calf milk replacer. I don't know if you'll like it or not," he said, shaking the bottle, "but we've got to get some sort of nutrition in you." He shook the bottle. With two fingers, he parted the colt's lips and tried to slip the rubber nipple into his mouth.

The colt jerked away, clamping his mouth shut. Ugh, what was that awful taste, hard and rubbery?

"Come on, little one. Give it a chance. There's milk inside."

The colt pressed his mouth shut tighter. He turned his head this way and that way. What was this man doing to him?

Arthur's fingers pried again, forcing the clamped jaw wide. He squeezed milk from the bottle, dribbling it onto the tiny pink tongue.

The colt's eyes opened wide as he felt the milk touch his parched tongue. Reflex made him swallow. The liquid tasted odd, not at all like his mother's milk and not like something he wanted to drink. He blew out his nostrils and milk exploded into the air.

Arthur jumped away from the spray, and then calmly tried again. "No snorting," he admonished. "This will warm your tummy and make your legs strong again."

Arthur worked for the better part of an hour. Sometimes it seemed they were wasting more than the colt drank, but little by little the colt absorbed the first nutrition he'd had in a few days. When Arthur finally stopped, they were both exhausted, but the man was not finished yet.

Arthur pulled a tube of ointment and a roll of bandage from his pocket. He squeezed medicine on the leg wound and then wrapped the bandage around and around, pinning it in place. He sat back and patted the foal.

The colt shook his leg. The bandage felt funny. He jiggled it hard, but a pain shot through his leg. He tried to ignore the pesky white attachment, turning his attention to Arthur instead. He nibbled at the man's pocket.

"You're a funny little boy," Arthur said, standing. "You rest awhile, now." He left the stall, promising to be back. "Cynthia will help me take care of you in the morning. My little girl is going to love you," he said.

The colt stretched out on his side and closed his eyes. He pictured his momma nudging him gently. In his mind, he suckled and felt the warm liquid she offered slide over his tongue. He inhaled her scent and switched his little tail at the mosquitoes in his dream. Slipping away from the memory that she was gone, the colt finally slept.

Courtesy of Carol Gazunis.

Chapter Four

Scratch, scratch, scratch!

The colt raised his head and looked around the stall.

Morning sun streamed through the tiny window in the high corner of the barn. The light was bright white, not thick and golden like the moonlight.

Scratch, scratch, scratch.

The mouse was at it again. The colt could see her pushing bits of broken straw and wood chips around a thick nest of fur in the corner. The fur wiggled. The nest was full of hairless baby mice.

The colt lifted his head and rolled upward from his side. He stretched out his forelegs and scrambled to stand, pushing simultaneously with long back legs. The milk had given him a tad more strength and he launched himself upward onto four shaky legs.

His head swam and everything blurred. Soon, though, his vision cleared and he took a wobbly step forward. The mouse scurried to cover her babies, pushing fur over them, hiding them in the straw.

The colt took another step, lowered his head to sniff the mice, and then stepped toward the stall door. He leaned forward, pushing his chest against the half door and stretching his neck long to see outside. The grass was green and vibrant. Flowers bloomed along the fence line. Out on the tip of the island, where blue bay waters met land, a small herd of ponies moved as one, noses buried in salty marsh cord grass. Memories flooded back.

The colt leaned into the gate and whinnied, a high-pitched squeal that made the ponies in the distance throw their heads up in the air to look. One mare, a palomino pinto with a broad white face, had a foal at her side. She trotted forward to the fence and her chestnut foal skedaddled along behind her.

A door slammed.

The colt heard voices and he recognized one of them. Arthur!

The second voice was small and light. It floated on the air like a butterfly. "What does he look like, Daddy? Is he a bay, a pinto, or chestnut? Can he be mine?"

Arthur laughed. "He's a tri-color, honey… a bay pinto, and no, you can't keep him. He belongs to the herds on the island. You know that the Chincoteague Fire Company owns the wild Chincoteague ponies."

"But you rescued him! You should be allowed to keep him," she sniffed.

"I don't even know if we can save him, let alone keep him," Arthur said. "He's pretty dang weak, an orphan with a bad leg and a bad eye. He's as skinny as a Halloween skeleton. If we don't get him to eat, he's gonna be a goner. Let's take one step at a time."

The colt strained to listen. They were closer. What does that mean? the colt wondered. What's a goner? I'm not a goner.

"But he drank milk for you, right?" The girl was persistent.

Arthur snorted. "I'd hardly say he drank milk. More like, I forced it down his throat."

"Didn't he like it?"

Arthur sighed. "You are so full of questions, Cynthia. No, he didn't like it. He fought me tooth and nail all the way. Half of it was wasted. We have to come up with a better way to get milk in him if he's to live."

There was silence then, just the crunch, crunch, crunch of gravel as they walked down the driveway toward the barn.

"What about old Sandy?" Cynthia asked softly. "She could nurse him."

Who is old Sandy? the colt wondered.

Arthur sighed. "We can give it a try," he said, "but you know Sandy's a cantankerous old mare. She won't cotton to the idea of a strange foal drinking her filly's milk."

They were only steps away now and the colt whinnied, a soft rumble meant to tell Arthur he was happy to see him. "Well now, look at who's standing," the man said, smiling broadly.

Cynthia stretched over the stall door. "Ooooh, he's so tiny," she said, "and beautiful." Her fingers touched the colt's nose as he backed away. She opened the stall door and they both went inside.

Arthur slipped a halter onto the foal and buckled it. "Hold him for me," he said, kneeling in the straw.

The colt rolled his eyes, trying to look at the halter. *What is on my face?*

While Cynthia held the colt, Arthur removed the bandage from his back leg. As it stripped away from the wound, the stench rose like an ominous cloud.

"Oh, Daddy, that's awful," Cynthia said, clapping her hand to her nose.

"It's pretty bad," he agreed. "We're gonna have to get Doc Cameron out here."

Another head appeared outside the stall — an older man who was as big as Arthur, but had a thick shock of white hair. "What have you gotten yourself into, son?" the old man asked.

The colt backed away and Arthur stood. There were too many strangers. The girl was one thing. She was small and seemed harmless, but who was this big man?

"Well, Dad, I couldn't leave him out there to die, could I?" Arthur responded.

Sunlight glinted off the colt's chocolate brown hair, adding reddish tints. "He practically matches you," the big man said. "He's a little Arthur."

"That's what I'm going to call him," Cynthia said, laughing. "Little Arthur!" Her laugh turned to a giggle. Saying her dad's name out loud seemed to amuse her. "After all, he has to have a name," she added.

"All right, then," Arthur said. "Now we have to get Little Arthur to eat something."

"What do you have in mind?" the big man asked.

Arthur stepped toward the door and shrugged. "I was going to ask you."

The big man ran a hand through his white hair. "Why don't you give Sandy a try," he suggested.

Cynthia smiled. "That was my idea, Pop Pop!"

The old man reached into the stall and tousled Cynthia's hair. "Great minds think alike," he said.

While she pondered that, the colt sidled up to her, pushing a frail face against her pants leg.

Arthur smiled and dropped his hand to scratch the fuzzy black stubble of a mane. "He sure was quick to trust us," he said.

Cynthia giggled. "You never get excited about new foals, Daddy, but you like him, don't you?"

"Well, I grew up with horses," Arthur explained, "so they don't excite me like they do you, but this one is different. He's special."

Cynthia ran a finger down the vivid white blaze. The colt reached up and brushed velvety lips against her fingertips.

Arthur smiled. "Yeah, he's won me over," he admitted. "But I'm easy. Now, let's hope he wins Sandy over, too."

Chapter Five

Cynthia rubbed the colt's neck. "Easy there, Little Arthur." She smiled as she said his name. "We're going to get you better."

Arthur lifted the colt's head in his hands. He looked at first one eye and then the other. He parted the eyelid to look into the sore eye, wiping away pus in the corner with a fingertip. He swiped his hand down his pants leg. "I think that'll heal up with some meds," he said.

Cynthia leaned in to get a better look. "I hope so."

"You keep him company while I get Sandy from the field," her dad said.

Little Arthur leaned his head against the girl's shoulder. He liked her. She was quiet and she had kind hands like her dad. Her blonde hair was long with silky waves and her blue eyes were as round and blue as Arthur's.

A black fly zoomed around the top of the stall and then lined up for a landing on the colt's back. He heard it coming and shuddered, but just before it could land, Cynthia's hand swept through the air and sent it sailing. "Stay away from Little Arthur," she ordered. Her voice was firm, but not loud. She patted the colt. "We're going to take care of you, boy."

Little Arthur puffed up with happiness. Outside, he could hear the foal in the meadow whinnying and calling frantically. The colt pushed past Cynthia to stick his head out the stall door. He leaned sideways to watch the chestnut filly race back and forth along the fence line. She had four white legs and a star in the middle of her forehead. She didn't look anything like her momma, the buckskin pinto mare.

Arthur walked toward them with the filly's momma. Sandy swung her head around again and again to check on her foal, almost sweeping the rope from Arthur's hand. She whinnied, a trembling loud call that made the colt jump sideways.

"Come on, now," Arthur warned the mare. "You won't be gone long and that little gal of yours is big enough to be on her own a minute or two. You won't even be out of her sight."

Cynthia reached for the lead rope hooked on the outside of the stall door. She opened the snap and clipped it on Little Arthur's halter. "Do you want me to lead him out?"

"No, no, no!" her dad said. "He's not like our other foals. That colt is wild, straight off the island. He hasn't learned how to lead yet. You stay put."

Cynthia ran a hand over the ridge of the colt's black mane. "Oh, yeah, you're a WILD thing," she said, smiling. "Crazy wild!"

Arthur snorted. "You didn't see him in the marsh last night, smarty pants." Arthur's smile warmed his words. "Unhook that lead rope, come out of there, and run up to the house to get your mom. I'm gonna need her help, too," he said.

Cynthia scrunched up her face. "I'm not a baby. I'm ten years old now. Let me help you... Please?"

Cynthia knew that mares don't normally nurse foals that are not their own. In fact, Sandy could actually hurt the colt if she wanted, but Cynthia was sure she could handle the colt. He was only a whisper of a thing and weak at that.

Arthur studied his daughter's face. The filly nickered in the background and the mare rumbled a low response.

"I've been helping you with foals on the farm for as long as I can remember, Dad. Doesn't that count for anything?" Her eyes pleaded along with her voice, softening Arthur's resolve.

"All right," he relented. "Open the stall door, but don't bring him out. I'm going to sidle Sandy up next to the barn. That way the colt will be able to reach her to nurse, but if she kicks at him, she'll most likely hit the side of the barn."

Cynthia swung the door wide, hooking it on the side of the barn to keep it in place.

The colt stood at the end of the rope, eyeing the mare. He moved forward to the edge of the doorway, but he didn't step out. His nose stretched long toward the mare. He snorted and hopped on his bad leg, and then pranced in place, but something kept him from bolting forward, maybe instinct, maybe common sense.

Arthur brought the mare closer. She grunted and threw her head into the air, coming up on hind legs. With a jerk of the lead rope, Arthur pulled her back. "Settle down," he said firmly. "Be nice."

Sandy was almost within reach of the colt when her filly whinnied again. She swung her head sideways and tore the lead rope from Arthur's hand. Her neck snaked forward, aiming for the colt and her teeth snapped together.

Cynthia saw the mare coming and jerked Little Arthur backward, saving him from a sharp bite.

That's two bites she's saved me from, the colt thought, remembering the fly.

Arthur had the mare under control again. "She caught me off-guard, but she won't get her head around this time," he said. "I'm going to back her closer. Are you ready?"

Cynthia nodded and gripped the lead rope, her other hand on the colt's halter.

Arthur backed the mare in. Her hind hooves were against the barn and she stood angled toward the door.

Cynthia clicked her tongue. "Come on, boy. You'll have to step out a little to reach her."

The colt's lower lip trembled. He could smell milk, real milk! His tummy rumbled and he stepped forward. He stretched his lips out, grazing the mare's side gently, leaning toward her udder.

Quicker than a woodpecker's peck the mare's hind legs shot out. Crash! Her hooves thundered as they made contact with the side of the barn. It all happened so fast. Arthur shouted and yanked her forward. Cynthia silently jumped back, pulling the colt into the stall again.

"Dang it, Sandy!" Arthur's voice was laced with frustration. "What in tarnation is wrong with you that you would try to hurt an itty bitty colt like that?"

Cynthia pulled Little Arthur close and rubbed his chest. She could feel his heart beating wildly. "It's okay," she soothed. "It's okay, little boy."

Arthur circled the mare. "You did a good job there, Cynthia," he said, "a much better job than old Sandy."

The colt felt a glow emanate from Cynthia. "What now, Dad?" she asked.

"I just got an idea," he said. "Could you skedaddle over to the feed room and bring back a rope and a bucket of grain, the kind with sweet molasses mixed in?"

"Sure, Dad." Cynthia unhooked the lead rope. "I'll be right back," she told the colt. He watched her slip out the door and dash to the little building next door. She was back in a flash with a bucket and a long coil of rope that she handed to her dad. "Whatcha gonna do?"

"Watch and see," he answered.

Arthur set the bucket of grain on the ground and then moved the mare away from it. He lifted her left hind leg in the air, ran a rope around her neck, and back to the leg he had lifted. He tied the rope to the leg. Poor Sandy was standing on three legs, one rear leg tied up. "Bring the colt out here and slide that bucket of grain over to me."

Cynthia walked out the door and the colt followed as if he'd already been trained to lead. He trusted this girl and he was sticking by her side. Cynthia used her boot to slide the bucket toward her dad, who lifted it to Sandy's nose.

The mare burrowed her face into the bucket, chomping down on sugared grain. While she ate, her ears flicked back and forth, listening to her filly, and then flattening for the colt, as if he were a monster...or an archenemy of the highest caliber.

"Get that colt in to nurse while her nose is busy," Arthur commanded.

Cynthia brought the colt close. He hesitated and then dove in to drink great gulps of milk, sweet as honey. Cynthia smiled. "Smart move, Dad," she said.

Her dad grinned. "A three-legged horse can't kick without falling over," he said.

Cynthia nodded. "And Sandy never could resist grain with molasses."

Courtesy of Brenda Boonie.

CHAPTER SIX

That evening, the colt slept with the first full belly he'd had in days. In the morning, Arthur brought the mare again. Sandy bulked. She stomped and reared and kicked, fighting the whole way, but Arthur was firm.

"I bet you're hungry," Cynthia told Little Arthur, scratching his ears. She held the lead rope tight and stroked his face and neck.

The colt stretched and danced when the mare approached. He knew she could hurt him if she tried, but he was hungry and the sweet memory of honeyed milk rolled around in his mind.

Arthur tied the mare's leg up again and offered the bucket of grain. Cynthia led the colt closer, but this time the mare was aggressive. Even though she couldn't kick, she hopped sideways, rotating with her nose in the bucket, knocking the colt away with her body.

Little Arthur had suckled, pulling a swallow from the teat before she banged him away.

Arthur jerked at Sandy's lead. She threw her head up and oats went flying. Arthur grabbed the bucket and grumbled at the mare, but gave the half empty pail back to her a moment later to try again.

This time, Little Arthur suckled fast and furious, closing his eyes while warm liquid flowed into his tummy, and then it happened again. In a flash, he was flung aside by the mare that slammed her body into him full force. He stumbled sideways.

Cynthia caught Little Arthur before he lost his balance. "Easy there," she said, pulling the colt to her gently.

"Dang it, Sandy!" Arthur was clearly frustrated. He yanked the rope, pulling the mare's head around. She hopped sideways on three legs, reaching out to nip at Arthur's arm. He jerked away.

"Well, she's never done that before," he said. "I do believe we've ticked her off." He turned to Cynthia. "Dad bought some milk replacer pellets yesterday," he said. "Would you mind working with the colt today to try to get him to eat them? I don't know how much longer Sandy will tolerate this."

Cynthia leaned into the foal. "Yes," she said and her voice was breathy and happy. "That would be fun."

Little Arthur's heart sank when Arthur led the mare away. Even though she had frightened him, her milk was warm and satisfying, and this time his tummy was nowhere near full.

The colt closed his eyes, remembering how his momma had reached down to lick the tips of his ears and how she'd pushed her brown spotted body close, nosing him toward her milk. He also recalled how she had groomed him with her tongue while he suckled. He sighed, missing her.

Cynthia led the colt into his stall. She turned him loose and then set about cleaning out the wet and dirty straw, carrying it from the stall with her mucking fork, piling it under the tall pine tree outside. She had just begun to spread fresh, earthy scented, golden straw when Arthur returned with a bucket of supplies.

"Let's get his wound cleaned up," he said.

"Is it going to smell again?" Cynthia wrinkled her nose.

"Probably," he said matter-of-factly. "I just hope it's getting better."

Cynthia held the colt's halter while her dad rolled the bandage from the leg. He peeled away the medicated pad. The stench that rose seemed worse than the day before.

"It smells like his leg is rotting," Cynthia said. She gagged and covered her nose with her hand.

The long-festering wound spread down the inside of the

colt's front leg from the knee joint to his fetlock, red and inflamed, oozing yellow pus.

Arthur wrapped a clean bandage onto the leg and stood up. "I'm going to call Doc Cameron," he said. "This thing isn't getting any better." He handed Cynthia a bucket. "There's milk pellets in here. See if you can get him to eat."

But Cynthia didn't get a chance. After he left, the foal sank to the stall floor at her feet. He was so tired he could hardly keep his eyes open.

Cynthia sat down beside Little Arthur, gently rubbing his shoulder. "Go ahead," she said, "sleep." She stretched her legs out beside him. "Babies need lots of naps."

Little Arthur laid his head on her lap and snorted with pleasure. He rolled his eyes upward to gaze at her through thick, dark lashes. Absolute contentment washed over him.

Over in the corner, the mouse burrowed into her nest with her babies, away from the girl's watchful eyes. Cynthia stroked the colt's black forelock and then his mane, scratching her way down his neck to where the mane became white.

Soon, Little Arthur's eyes closed. He snored softly while Cynthia stroked his neck and traced the blaze on his long dark face.

CHAPTER SEVEN

By the time Doc Cameron came late that evening, the setting sun bathed the 58-acre Chincoteague Pony Farm in golden light. As the truck pulled into the driveway, pine trees cast their shadowed branches upon the ground. Silhouettes of trees and bushes swayed in checkered patterns on the lawn.

The colt watched the truck approach from his post at the stall door. He listened to the crunch of gravel and watched Cynthia trot to greet the man, followed by her dad. He whinnied when they turned to head his way. She heard him and took off running for the barn, leaving the men behind.

"Hey, squirt!" she blurted when she reached Little Arthur. She was breathless and smiling and the colt rumbled a soft greeting of his own.

"Go ahead and bring him out, Cynthia," Dad called.

She reached around the corner to get the lead rope and stepped inside the stall to clip it to Little Arthur's halter. Then she led him out.

Little Arthur lowered his head to grab at tufts of grass as they walked. Even though he hadn't yet learned he could survive on it, the colt loved the tangy taste of each slender blade when he rolled it in his mouth and gnashed with his little teeth.

Cynthia stopped to wait for the men. The colt alternated between nibbling grass and raising his head to watch them approach.

Charlie Cameron wore royal blue coveralls and carried a leather bag. He was tall with wire-framed glasses that perched on his nose. The colt watched him approach. The man had a smile that surfaced from time to time as he walked and talked. Little Arthur relaxed. The man didn't seem scary at all. So far, humans had been good to him and the colt was learning to trust.

"Hey, little guy," Doc Cameron said, reaching to stroke his side.

The colt stood stock still, leaning into Cynthia, watching every move the man made.

"He's frail," he said.

Arthur nodded. "We're working on that. He got a few meals from Sandy, but she wasn't cooperative. Cynthia's working on getting him to eat milk pellets."

"He did pretty well today," Cynthia said. "He ate several handfuls. He won't eat from the bucket, but he nibbled them from my hand."

Doc Cameron nodded. "That's good. You keep working at it and he'll be eating out of the bucket in no time at all."

The doc took the colt's head in his hand, and looked at the eye. "He's got a little abscess there, but that's already starting to heal."

"I've been rubbing antibacterial cream in the eye," Arthur said.

Doc Cameron bent over to rummage in his bag and his hand came out with a different tube of ointment. "Try this," he said, "twice a day. It should clear up fast."

Arthur nodded. "It's the leg I'm worried about," he said.

Cynthia knelt down to unwrap the bandage from the colt's leg. "I'll get it," she said.

The colt felt the doctor run a hand down his back leg. The man lifted it gently to examine the wound.

"This is not good," the vet said. "The infection is deep into the leg."

The colt felt something cold and wet. He snorted and hopped sideways. Pain seared its way up his leg.

"Easy there, boy." Cynthia folded herself into the foal, standing as close as possible, rubbing his neck to distract him as the doctor cleaned the wound.

The colt did not know what they were doing to his leg. Whatever it was, it felt cold and wet and brought waves of pain.

He snorted and hopped to his left three times.

The veterinarian was patient. He waited for the foal to calm before touching the leg again and then he scraped at the infection, working to clear the pus and dried blood.

Little Arthur tried to jerk his leg away, but Doc Cameron held tight. Soon the man was slathering ointment onto the wound and wrapping it again.

The colt was used to the feel of the bandage on his leg by now. He relaxed as the vet stepped away to root in his bag. Suddenly, without notice, the man plunged something pointy into his neck. Pain shot through the colt and he reared up on his hind legs. Before he was down again, the pain was gone.

"Whoa boy," Cynthia said, holding tight to the lead rope.

"That needle will attack the infection," Doc Cameron said. "I don't know what the odds are for this little fellow, though. That's a deep infection. It'll take some powerful antibodies to fight it." He picked up the paper trash from the needle's packaging and the bandage wrapping and closed his bag before standing. "Only time will tell."

Cynthia stayed with the colt. The pair watched the men walk away. "Do you want to nibble some grass?" she asked.

The colt didn't know what she'd said. He only knew that she was leading him toward the grassy part of the yard. He lowered his head to grab tufts of thick juicy green between baby teeth. The white bandage on his leg stood out as bright as the moon that now rose in the sky. Evening mosquitoes buzzed about his fuzzy ears, but he didn't pay them any mind. Here was grass, and the girl, and the peaceful sound of tree frogs chirping.

Cynthia rubbed a hand along the colt's backbone and sat down in the soft grass and pine needle bed under the largest Loblolly pine in the yard. As the colt grazed, he made sure she was never out of sight.

Courtesy of Lisa Damsgaard.

Chapter Eight

Sometime during the night, Little Arthur awoke in his stall. The mouse was scratching in the corner, but that wasn't what had awakened him. The pain in his leg had grown sharp, slipping into his dreams and stirring him from sleep.

He scrambled to his hooves and worked his way to the water bucket, where he lowered his head to pull long draughts of water. When he raised his head at last, water dripped from his whiskery muzzle. The waning moon was slimmer, but still bright in the sky. Its light slipped between the cracks of the barn and carved a silvery path from the open top half of the stall door, across the straw to where he stood.

The colt gingerly stepped toward the door, hopping to keep his weight off the bad leg. He felt like he was on fire, especially the leg. Cool night air brushed against his face when he stretched his nose over the door. It made him feel chilly and hot all at the same time.

The foal circled in the stall, head down, shoveling his nose through the straw in agitation. The little mouse scampered in front of his feet toward her nest again, pushing more straw around her babies, as if to protect them from the colt's milling legs.

Finally, the colt folded his legs and lowered his aching body into the straw. He slept in fits and spurts, dreaming of Assateague Island, of water stretching out for miles, of a herd far in the distance, leaving him behind. He snorted in his sleep...and then felt the touch of a hand on his forehead.

"He's really hot, Dad!"

The colt's eyes flew open. It was morning and Cynthia was there. He grumbled low in his throat. It was half greeting, half complaint. He wanted the girl to take away the heat in his body and the pain that pulsed in his leg. Arthur bent over the colt, who watched them both through heavily lidded eyes.

"He's going downhill," he said. "I'll call Doc."

The door clicked shut when Arthur stepped out, leaving Cynthia behind to stroke Little Arthur's head and whisper quiet meaningless words that eased his racing thoughts, calming the parade of pictures going through his mind.

Cynthia waited in the early morning light with Arthur. He watched the shadow of her arm blend with other checkered shadows on the stall floor. She petted him from the tip of his ears and down his back to the start of his tail, again and again. It was soothingly hypnotic. He closed his eyes again, falling into dark realms of sleep.

When he was jarred awake again, Doc Cameron and Arthur were both there. He tried to shake away their blurred images, but the veterinarian's hand was firm on his neck. He felt a rectal thermometer go in under his tail.

Doc Cameron pulled the thermometer out. "104," he said. "He's a sick one."

"What's a normal temperature?" Cynthia asked. "I know humans should be 98.6, but what's normal for a horse?"

"99 to 101," Doc Cameron replied. He wiped the thermometer off with a medical wipe and put it back in his bag. "104 is not good."

The colt felt the sharp prick of another needle. He was so exhausted he barely moved when this needle went in.

"I've given him a stronger antibiotic." Doc Cameron snapped his bag shut. "There's a muscle relaxer in it and he may be drowsy. Make sure he gets plenty of water until this fever drops."

Arthur nodded.

"I'll take care of him," Cynthia spoke up. "Can I stay out here with him all morning, Dad?"

"I don't think that's a good idea," he answered. "Mom will be waiting with breakfast."

"But..."

"Let me walk the doc back to his truck," Arthur interrupted.

"I'll talk to you in a minute."

The colt heard the two men walk up the drive. Their voices echoed in the quiet morning and their boots clicked with every step. Back and forth the voices went.

"I bet they're talking about you," Cynthia said. She rubbed his aching muscles and spoke in soft tones. "I hope they figure something out." Her voice brimmed with worry. "They have to get you well."

He heard the gravel crunch when the truck pulled out of the driveway, and then Arthur was back.

"Honey, you have to come in for breakfast, but you can come back out and spend the whole morning with him if you like."

Little Arthur tried to stand up when Cynthia did. He didn't want her to leave. He heaved himself up and stood shakily. He wanted to tell her to stay, but he wasn't sure he could whinny and keep his balance. He swayed dizzily, and then decided he was better off resting. He crumbled into the straw again, lifted his head, and watched her leave.

"I'll be back, little one," she said. "Don't you worry, I'll be back."

The colt slept then. His breath came in deep whooshes. The erratic dreams were gone and a solid, restful sleep overtook him. The antibiotics were working on the infection and the relaxers were helping him get the rest he needed to heal.

When he awoke, hours later, Cynthia was there. She had stretched out beside him on a pink and blue checkered sleeping bag, her arm thrown across his midsection. It was sunny, the afternoon at least, but her eyes were closed.

When she felt him stir, the girl's hand came to life, rubbing, scratching, and massaging his achy muscles.

He couldn't see her face behind his back, but he watched her hand move. He felt the same love in her hands that he'd felt in his mother's touch and he knew he was safe.

CHAPTER NINE

Over the next few weeks, Doc Cameron came and went. Cynthia spent most of her days with Little Arthur. He had learned to gobble up the pellets she brought him. He sucked up the cool, clean water brought to his bucket daily through a long green hose. He felt himself grow stronger.

The colt watched for Cynthia every morning and knew she would return again after lunch. Although his eye had healed, the leg continued to fester, the infection sloughing the hair and skin from his leg in a zigzag pattern. Some days brought fever. On others, the colt felt spunky and full of zest.

"You need exercise," Cynthia said on one of the good days. "Let's get out of this stall and walk the property line."

Little Arthur hopped along behind her as she held onto the lead rope. Cynthia walked slowly, allowing the colt to take his time. They followed a line of fragrant pine trees and tall oaks. The sun moved in and out among the clouds. One minute the sky grew dark and gray and the next the sun shone brightly.

They passed chickens pecking their way along, their heads bobbing into the grass again and again. The red bandy hens cackled and buck-bucked their way along, oblivious to the colt that had lowered his head to sniff at feathers left behind.

"You are so curious," Cynthia said. "Those are chickens. They give us eggs for breakfast and for cakes and cookies, some of the treats I bring you!"

Little Arthur stared at her quizzically, trying to understand the words. He followed when she left the treeline and walked along the fence toward the water. The ponies on the other side, inside the fence, raced back and forth beside them, nickering and calling out. Only Old Sandy kept her distance. She'd had enough of the colt, he imagined.

A bay filly was at the fence, pushing away from her mother, neighing to Little Arthur. The filly pranced back and forth, wanting to meet the colt.

The colt pulled on the lead rope and Cynthia allowed him to stretch closer, to sniff the filly's velvety black muzzle. She snorted and her eyes went wide. She had dark, long, lashes that curled, forming a frame around each wide eye. Little Arthur danced in place, delighted.

"I bet that leg feels better when there's a pretty little filly to flirt with," Cynthia said with a laugh. "That filly is Moony!" She led him away, down to the sandy beach.

Little Arthur gazed out over the waters of the bay. In the distance he could see Assateague Island. The gulls dipped and called out, "Cray, cray," and across the way a tall blue heron picked her way through the marshes of Assateague. Something told him that island was his home, that was where he belonged, and he pulled at the lead rope, dancing near the lapping edge of the water.

Cynthia laughed again. "You can prance into the water all you want," she said, "but you are not ready to go home."

Little Arthur hung his head into the water, blowing air, making bubbles. He pawed at the sand until a fiddler crab poked his head out of a hole and scurried away, burrowing himself into another hole in no time at all.

Cynthia plunked down in the sand, allowing the colt to play in the water on his long lead rope. He pawed at the lapping liquid awhile, sending spray upward, and then turned back to the girl, watching her gaze out over the bay across the way to Assateague Island.

Now and again the colt circled on the lead rope to join Cynthia. He raised his head high and sniffed the breeze that blew in from the island across the way. His nostrils flared and his eyes widened.

Later that evening, after they'd returned to the stall, Arthur came to check on his daughter and the colt.

"How's he doing?"

"His fever is gone," Cynthia said, "and his eye looks better... but look at his leg." She shook her head. "It looks just awful."

Arthur went down on one knee, working the bandage from the colt's leg. As it came off, the rotting smell filled the air again. "Phew, it's dreadful." Her dad shook his head. "I know you don't want to hear this, Cynthia, but this may not heal."

Cynthia knelt down beside her dad.

Little Arthur ruffled her hair with his nose.

"Do you mean he could die?" Her voice was somber and sad. Little Arthur lowered his head to gaze at her face. She stroked the white on his nose.

Arthur stood up. "I just don't know what to tell you," he said. His words were laced with frustration. "We've tried everything. We've thrown every medicine the doc can think of at that infection and it hasn't gotten one bit better."

"What does Doc Cameron say about it?" Cynthia asked. Her voice went up a notch.

"Well, he did suggest one more thing, but it's kind of gross and he said it's not recommended."

Little Arthur sidled closer to Cynthia, rooting in her palm, looking for a treat.

"What?" Cynthia stood stock still, waiting for him to answer.

"He suggested we try something that was done to soldiers back in the Civil War days, an odd remedy that will either cure him or kill him."

Dad stepped out the stall door and Cynthia followed. She snapped the door shut behind her, lowering the latch in place. The colt wondered why she was ignoring him. "What.... What is it? Is it worth a try?"

"It will look a lot worse before it gets better... that is, if it works at all," Arthur said. "The doc said a last measure would be to take the bandages off, let the air get to it, stop the medicines and..."

"And what?"

"Let the flies lay their eggs in the bloody mess."

"What?!"

Cynthia's shrill voice made the colt nervous. He leaned against the door, rubbing his neck back and forth on the wooden frame. She reached over and stroked his head and shoulder, calming him.

"When fly eggs hatch, maggots come out. The maggots will eat away the infection."

"Does that really work?" Cynthia's voice was incredulous. She rubbed Little Arthur's neck harder, scratching for all she was worth.

"Sometimes," Dad said. "During the war, many men were saved when maggots ate away their infection. Sometimes, though, the maggots brought even more infection. There's a fifty percent chance it will heal his leg. There's a fifty percent chance he will die."

Cynthia blinked back tears while her dad scratched his beard and nodded.

"I don't know what to tell you, honey," he said. "We've tried everything else. If the infection isn't brought under control soon, it could get in his bloodstream and kill him."

Tears rolled down Cynthia's cheek. She turned her back to her dad and faced the colt. She cradled his head in her hands. "You have to get better," she whispered to him. "You have to make yourself get better."

Chapter Ten

The foal stood motionless, his head stretched over the half door into the dark. He watched ribbons of moonlight ripple on the surface of the bay. He loved how peaceful the moon made him feel and it had become his practice to stand at the door late at night.

An owl called out, his hoot, hoot penetrating the soundless night. Deer hooves rustled dry needles as their slender brown bodies passed under the line of pine trees that followed the fence line. Tonight, the colt was restless.

Cynthia and her dad had peeled away the bandages, leaving his sore leg open to the air. Those bandages had covered his wound for weeks now. They'd become a part of him. Now he felt exposed, like something was missing that should be there. He stamped his hoof impatiently.

The bay filly followed her momma across the pasture down near the water, two shadows moving in unison.

Little Arthur felt more alone than he had in quite some time. He was used to his leg throbbing, but there was a new feeling now. Flies surrounded the wound, buzzing, landing, crawling, tickling, until he had to stamp his hoof again. The movement only caused them to take flight momentarily before lighting again; tickling paths up and down the sore leg.

Little Arthur paced circles around his stall, coming back to the doorway again and again. A red fox slipped between the outbuildings, silently heading out the lane.

Finally, the colt buckled his legs and lowered himself onto the bedding to rest. He rolled, stretching his neck and head out into the soft straw. Behind his ear he heard the baby mice moving in their nest and he felt a little less alone. The babies had hair now and peeked out of the nest from time to time, raising their heads above the straw to look around. The mother mouse scurried past and then stopped to rise up on her hind legs and stare at him, her whiskers twitching. The colt sighed and finally slept.

A ray of morning sun stretched across the stall like a shadow in reverse, sliding over Little Arthur, lighting his back legs and then his midsection, moving up his neck and warming his fur. When the light tickled its way across the colt's face, he finally opened his eyes and snorted, sending pieces of straw dust upward to dance with dust motes in the sunny stall.

The first thing the colt noticed was that his leg no longer throbbed. It burned and itched and felt like a million tiny insects were racing up and down the wound, but the painful throb had disappeared. He pulled himself up to his feet and immediately had to stomp.

It felt like a colony of ants marched under the skin of the hairless leg. He stomped again to chase away the maddening itch and when that didn't work he circled the stall frantically, working his way up to a bucking trot. Dust rose to his nostrils. He kicked out with his hind legs and then stamped again, but nothing he did could stop the crazy buzz of activity racing up and down his leg.

When Cynthia finally came, she found him standing in the middle of his stall, head hanging. He reached back from time to time to nip at the burdensome leg. She ran a hand over his neck and he melted toward her, soaking in the warmth and gentle touch of her fingers.

"Come on, boy," she said. "Let's get you out of this stall for a bit." She snapped on a lead rope and opened the door to lead him out into the sunny morning.

Outside the dusty stall, the air smelled of salt and pine and marshy things, pulling the colt's attention away from the bothersome leg. He stuck his nose into the air and whinnied at the ponies on the point. They raised their heads and bugled in return. The colt picked up his pace, dancing on his end of the lead rope.

Cynthia laughed and pulled him to a stop. In the bright morning light, she bent to examine the leg and then rose back again just as fast, coughing and blinking rapidly. "Ugh," she said. "Ah, that is just awful. Arh."

The colt froze in place. Never before had the girl jumped away from him in this fashion.

She buried her face in the ripple of mane on the crest of his neck. "I'm sorry boy," she whispered. She sighed. "The fly eggs have hatched and your leg is crawling with maggots." She coughed again. "Dad said it will make you better." She was quiet a moment and then she whispered, "You're going to get better." She said it with such resolve that Little Arthur believed it was true.

Their walk was a long one. Cynthia led the colt around the property, past the other ponies and the line of water that formed the point of the island. She let him prance on the end of the lead line as they turned to walk through the soft needled section of pines and out to the long driveway where Doc Cameron's truck traveled in and out of the farm. They moseyed along the edge of the lane, out to the road that led into town. Cynthia stopped to rest beside a gray stone marker, rubbing her fingers over the markings cut into the stone.

The colt pulled long shoots of honey-sweet grass from the sandy soil in mouthfuls, chewing slowly, savoring the flavor and staring down the roadway. From time to time a car or truck reached the circle that ended the road. Each time, Cynthia raised her hand to wave when they made the turn to head back into town. "Tourists," she told the colt, "out exploring the island. The road ends at our driveway so they have no choice but to turn around."

Cynthia and the colt relaxed together for quite some time, the foal grazing while Cynthia read from a book she'd pulled from her pocket. Whenever he looked at her, she'd stop to scratch him under his chin or along the neckline and the colt liked that. He leaned into her and closed his eyes, feeling the creepy crawlies race up and down his leg.

Courtesy of Sarah Boudreaux.

CHAPTER ELEVEN

"Dad, come quick! You have to see how much better this leg looks! You gotta see for yourself."

The colt watched Cynthia hop over his stall door and he thrust his head over it to see her race toward her father who was coming down the walkway from the house. She had bent to examine his leg just a moment before. Now she moved faster than an eastern cottontail rabbit, and he knew how fast they were. He'd seen plenty of them on Assateague Island.

Cynthia's dad was laughing when she caught up with him. Little Arthur watched her jump up and down with excitement, tugging at his arm.

The colt leaned his chest into the gate, yearning for her to return. His leg felt good today. There was no pain and the creepy crawly feeling had gone away.

Cynthia and her father stopped, their heads together in serious conversation. The colt turned from the door and paced impatiently, avoiding one corner of the stall. He could hear the baby mice rustling under the bedding. They'd grown in the past week and were scurrying around on their own these days, causing him to walk with more caution than ever before.

She swung the door open and tugged on the halter. Little Arthur stepped out of the stall, following her as she walked him down the driveway and back.

"See, he's not limping at all," she said, excitement back in her voice again. "And look at this!" She had stopped in front of her Dad and pointed to the rear leg that had once oozed with infection.

Her father knelt down, ran his hand down the leg, and whistled under his breath. "I can't believe how fast it healed up once we took the bandages off," he said. He straightened up and dropped a hand on Cynthia's shoulder. "You did a good job, honey."

Cynthia finger-combed the colt's mane and smiled. She scratched his neck, hitting all the itchy spots. He leaned into her hands and joy washed over him.

"Can we keep him?" Cynthia asked, and the colt knew she was talking about him.

"You know you can't," Dad said. "He belongs to the Fire Department, but even more, he belongs to the island."

"But we saved him!" She reached over the door to take the colt's head in her hands. He stared up at her blue eyes, waiting for the kiss he knew would land on his nose. When it came, he closed his eyes, feeling his lashes brush together, and then opened his eyes again. He loved her touch.

"And it was the right thing to do," Dad answered.

"He's going to be okay now, right Dad?"

Arthur laughed out loud. "I think he's going to be just fine." The colt felt the large man's eyes upon him. "He's a fine colt, too," he added. "One day he will make a magnificent herd sire."

A puzzled look crossed Cynthia's eyes, but only for a second, and then she said, "You mean he will have a herd of his own one day?"

"Yes, he will have a band of mares he'll call his own and he will father many strong foals to be sold at Pony Penning."

"Well, then," Cynthia said, "that settles it. I've been thinking about this anyway, but now I know we have to do it."

It was her dad's turn to look puzzled. "Just what is it we have to do?"

"Change his name." She sucked in a whoosh of breath. "Before you say no, just listen. The name Little Arthur is too plain and anyway one day he will be a big stallion and not a little Arthur. He needs a name that tells everyone what he's been through, a name that tells them how he beat the odds to become a real legend."

"I see," Dad said. "You want the world to know he survived something tough and he is a miracle." He chuckled. "You want everyone to know that he's the man of the island!"

"Exactly!"

Dad nodded slowly. "Okay, what do you think we should call him?"

Cynthia thought only a moment. "You just said it, Dad. He's a miracle, he really is... We should call him 'Miracle Man'."

AFTERWORD

Although the conversation in this book is imagined, the story of the colt Miracle Man is a true one. He was rescued by Arthur Leonard just as this book depicts. Arthur and his daughter, Cynthia, cared for the colt with the help of Doc Cameron until the bandages were removed and the leg miraculously healed.

When winter came, a decision was made to send the young colt to Florida to stay with the Leonard's good friend, Stan White. The warm weather of this southern state gave the colt more healing time without the added stress of the island's winter cold.

While in Florida, White taught the colt several tricks. When Miracle Man returned to Chincoteague Island in the summer of 1996, he was led into the ring at Pony Penning to meet the crowds at the world famous auction. He bowed in the center of the ring and gave kisses to a smiling young woman.

The Leonard family kept Miracle Man on their Chincoteague Pony Farm for several years as he grew to adulthood. When he was released on the island, he quickly claimed mares of his own and began to produce the fine strong foals predicted by Arthur Leonard.

In 2009, Miracle Man showed everyone his extreme intelligence. Cowboys had arrived on Chincoteague the weekend before the wild pony swim. They'd come to round up the ponies and pen them on Assateague, just as they have done for many years. Inside those pens other stallions often fight to protect and steal mares. They are held in the pens until the swim on the Wednesday of Pony Penning.

When Miracle Man saw the cowboys on horseback, he knew what was going to happen. He'd lived through over a decade of swims. He knew he didn't want to go into the holding pens on Assateague with all those other stallions, so he herded his mares into the bay and swam to Chincoteague. He came ashore at Memorial Park, where the pony swim always takes place, and then he herded his mares down the streets toward the carnival grounds.

When people arrived on Chincoteague for Pony Penning week, they found Miracle Man and his band of mares and foals already penned at the carnival grounds. This wise stallion knew just what he wanted to do and he did it. Miracle Man is truly an island legend.

Courtesy of Carol Gazunis.

Acknowledgments

I would like to acknowledge a number of people for their willingness to not only share Miracle Man's story, but also their help in getting dates and facts correct so that I could share the story of this legendary stallion.

I met Miracle Man as a foal in July of 1995 after seeing an article by Nancy Namoski in the *Chincoteague Beacon* newspaper. After calling Arthur Leonard, he welcomed me onto his family farm, introduced me to the injured and orphaned foal, and shared his story.

Years later, Cynthia Leonard not only verified facts, but willingly read the manuscript as a fact-checker.

Numerous individuals donated photos for possible inclusion into the book, including Lise Damsgaard, Brenda Boonie, Kris Barnes, Carol Gazunis, Tony Meyers, and Sarah Boudreax.

I would also like to thank all the individuals I've named above and the amazing Chincoteague Fire Department and their Pony Committee for all they do to keep these legendary ponies safe and well and available to the public.

Glossary

Island Terms:

Assateague Island: Assateague Island is a 33-mile-long island that lies along the coast of Maryland and Virginia. Wild ponies inhabit the island. On the Virginia side (the side that borders Chincoteague Island), Assateague is a wildlife refuge.

Chincoteague Island: An island off the coast of Virginia on the East Coast of the United States. The island is seven miles long and one and a half miles wide and is known for its harvest of seafood and the wild pony swim and auction that is held during the last week of July each year. Chincoteague was named by an early Indian Tribe; it means "beautiful land across the waters." Chincoteague Island is only four inches above sea level. If not for the barrier island of Assateague, Chincoteague Island would be washed away by the ocean!

Chincoteague Ponies: The Assateague Island ponies that live on the Virginia half of Assateague, which are fenced off from the ones on the Maryland side, are called the Chincoteague Ponies. The Chincoteague Volunteer Fire Department owns the Chincoteague Ponies and they have made a concentrated effort to improve the breed by introducing several other breeds into the herds, including Arabians and Mustangs. The resulting pony herds are just as hardy, but more refined. The Chincoteague Ponies now have a registry.

Pony Penning: Each year the Chincoteague Volunteer Fire Department rounds up all the ponies on the Virginia side of Assateague Island. These saltwater cowboys herd the ponies into the narrowest part of the bay at slack tide and swim them to Chincoteague Island, bringing them ashore at Memorial Park. After a brief rest, the ponies are paraded from Memorial Park to the Chincoteague Fire Department's carnival grounds. They always swim the last Wednesday of July and they are always auctioned off on the last Thursday of July, and then they are returned to the island of Assateague on Friday. This tradition began over three hundred years ago as a way of controlling herd size, but it became much more. Over the years it has become a fundraiser for the fire department, as well as a time of great fun and celebration. Pony Penning was made famous in 1947 when Marguerite Henry's famous children's book, *Misty of Chincoteague*, was published.

Sika Deer: Originally brought to the East Coast by Boy Scouts, Japanese elk, known as Sika deer, are a common sight on Chincoteague Island. They are much smaller than the Whitetail deer that are native to the area. Over eight hundred Sika Deer live on Chincoteague Island and they can often be seen grazing by the sides of the roads and trails.

Whitetail Deer: Whitetail deer are native to the East Coast. The Chincoteague Island Refuge is home to about two hundred Whitetail deer. They are shyer than the Sika deer that live on the refuge.

Equine Terms:

Colt: A boy foal.
Fetlock: The lower part of a horse's leg above and behind the hoof and covered with a tuft of hair.
Filly: A girl foal.
Foal: A baby horse or pony.
Forelock: The long hair that grows between the ears of a horse or pony and falls across their forehead.
Herd Sire: The stallion that leads his band of mares and is the father of the foals they produce.

Mane: The long hair that grows from the neck of a horse or pony from behind the ears to the start of the back.

Mare: A mature female horse or pony.

Pony: A horse that is under fourteen hands in height. Horses are measured from the highest point of the withers (high point of the back) to the ground. Each hand equals four inches.

Stallion: A mature male horse or pony that is still able to father young.

Tack: Equipment specifically for horses. Some of the most used tack includes saddles, bridles, halters, and saddle pads.

Tail: The long hair that grows from the back of a horse in the same way a puppy or a cat has a tail.

Yearling: A horse or pony that is one year old.

Chincoteague Pony Colors:

Bay: A dark brown horse or pony with a black mane and tail, nose, muzzle, and legs. The black is known as black tips. A bay horse may or may not have white legs or a white marking on the face.

Black: Solid black with a black mane and tail.

Chestnut: A reddish brown horse or pony with a flaxen, cream-colored, or reddish-colored mane and tail. Chestnut colored horses are often described as being the color of a new copper penny.

Palomino: A golden-colored horse with a cream or flaxen mane and tail.

Pinto: A pinto horse can be white with splotches of color (such as chestnut, bay, palomino, or black) or one of those colors with large spots of white. Chincoteague is known for their many flashy pinto ponies.

Roan: A solid-colored horse whose coloring is sprinkled with white hairs.

Sorrel: A light chestnut.

Pony Markings:

Star: A small white patch on the forehead of the horse between the eyes.

Stripe: A thin white line down the face of the horse.

Blaze: A wide strip of white down the face of the horse.

Bald Face: A wide blaze, extending to or past the eyes.

Snip: A small strip of color usually on the nose of the horse between the nostrils.

Stocking: A white leg marking that extends at least to the bottom of the knee or hock, sometimes higher.

Sock: A white leg marking that extends higher than the fetlock, but not as high as the knee or hock.

Boot: A white marking that extends over the fetlock and is slightly lower than a sock.

Pastern: A white marking that extends above the top of the hoof, but stops below the fetlock.

Coronet: A thin line of white around the leg, just above the hoof, around the coronary band. It is usually no more than one inch above the hoof.

Other Schiffer Books by the Author:
Wild Colt, 978-0-7643-3975-2, $16.99
Chincoteague Ponies: Untold Tails, 978-0-7643-4085-7, $24.99
The True Story of Sea Feather, 978-0-7643-3609-6, $14.99
Out of the Sea, Today's Chincoteague Pony, 978-0-8703-3595-2, $14.95
Chincoteague Pony Identification Cards, 978-0-7643-4453-4, $19.99

Type set in Garamond

ISBN: 978-0-7643-4420-6
Printed in China

Published by Schiffer Publishing, Ltd.
4880 Lower Valley Road
Atglen, PA 19310
Phone: (610) 593-1777; Fax: (610) 593-2002
E-mail: Info@schifferbooks.com

For our complete selection of fine books on this and related subjects, please visit our website at **www.schifferbooks.com**. You may also write for a free catalog.

This book may be purchased from the publisher. Please try your bookstore first.

We are always looking for people to write books on new and related subjects. If you have an idea for a book, please contact us at
proposals@schifferbooks.com.

Schiffer Publishing's titles are available at special discounts for bulk purchases for sales promotions or premiums. Special editions, including personalized covers, corporate imprints, and excerpts can be created in large quantities for special needs. For more information, contact the publisher.

In Europe, Schiffer books are distributed by
Bushwood Books
6 Marksbury Ave.
Kew Gardens
Surrey TW9 4JF England
Phone: 44 (0) 20 8392 8585; Fax: 44 (0) 20 8392 9876
E-mail: info@bushwoodbooks.co.uk
Website: www.bushwoodbooks.co.uk